Oh, the doors you will open!

HARCOURT SCHOOL PUBLISHERS

STORYtown

DISCARD

Zoom Along

Senior Authors

Isabel L. Beck • Roger C. Farr • Dorothy S. Strickland

Authors

Alma Flor Ada • Roxanne F. Hudson • Margaret G. McKeown
Robin C. Scarcella • Julie A. Washington

Consultants

F. Isabel Campoy • Tyrone C. Howard • David A. Monti

HOUGHTON
MIFFLIN
HARCOURT
School Publishers

HARCOURT SCHOOL PUBLISHERS

STORYtown

Zoom Along

HOUGHTON
MIFFLIN
HARCOURT
School Publishers

Theme 3
Turning Corners

Contents

Comprehension Strategies 8

Theme Opener 12

Lesson 7

Get Started Story

Social Studies

Ten Eggs 16

Phonics: Short Vowel <u>e</u> 24

Words to Know 26

Little Red Hen Gets Help 28
by Kenneth Spengler • illustrated by Margaret Spengler • FANTASY

Paired Selections

Let's Make Tortillas! 46
RECIPE

Social Studies

Connections 48

Theme Writing ▶ Reading-Writing Connection

.... 50
Student Writing Model: Describing an Event

Lesson 8

Get Started Story

Thanks, Seth! 54

Focus Skill **Details** 62

Words to Know 64

Beth's Job 66
by Carole Roberts • illustrated by Michael Garland • REALISTIC FICTION

Flowers Grow 88
NONFICTION

Connections 90

Science

Science

Paired Selections

Lesson 9

Get Started Story

A Nut Falls 94

Focus Skill **Details** 102

Words to Know 104

Plants Can't Jump 106
by Ned Crowley • NONFICTION

Cornfield Leaves 128
by Lessie Jones Little • POETRY

Connections 130

Science

Science

Paired Selections

Lesson 10

Social
Studies

Social
Studies

Get Started Story

Frog Gets His Song 134

Plot 142

Words to Know 144

Soccer Song 146
by Patricia Reilly Giff • illustrated by Blanche Sims • REALISTIC FICTION

Now You Know About Soccer 164
NONFICTION

Paired
Selections

Connections 166

Lesson 11

Science

Science

Get Started Story

Sid Scores 170

Words with or and ore 178

Words to Know 180

Land of Ice 182
by Norbert Wu • NONFICTION

Paired
Selections

My Father's Feet 204
by Judy Sierra • POETRY

Connections 206

Lesson 12

Social Studies

Get Started Story

Fox and His Big Wish 210

Focus Skill Setting 218

Words to Know 220

King Midas and His Gold 222

by Patricia and Fredrick McKissack • illustrated by Josée Masse • MYTH

Paired Selections

Gold and Money 244

NONFICTION

Connections 246

Glossary 248

Social Studies

Theme Big Books

"The Frog and the Ox"

Decodable Books 7–12

Before You Read

Look at the pictures. Think about what you already know.

While You Read

Ask questions.

What do frogs eat?

Reread.

I'll read this page again.

Answer questions.

Oh! Some frogs eat bugs.

After You Read

Summarize.

First, tadpoles hatch from eggs. Then, they begin changing into frogs. Last, they are full-grown frogs.

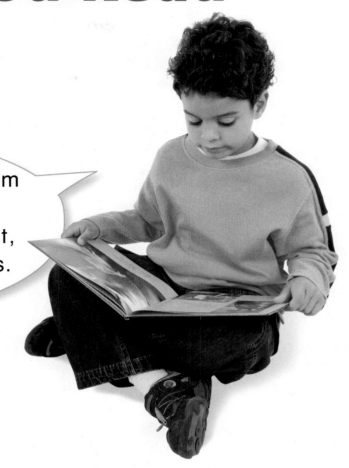

Make connections.

This is like another book I read. I learned about how butterflies change.

READING-WRITING
CONNECTION

	Lesson 7	Lesson 8	Lesson 9
Selection Titles	Ten Eggs **Little Red Hen Gets Help** Let's Make Tortillas!	Thanks, Seth! **Beth's Job** Flowers Grow	A Nut Falls **Plants Can't Jump** Cornfield Leaves
Comprehension Strategies	Answer Questions	Use Graphic Organizers	Reading Rate
Focus Skills	Short Vowel e	Details	Details

Theme ③ Turning Corners

The Gardeners, Judy Byford

Lesson 10 ▶

Frog Gets His Song
Soccer Song
Now You Know About Soccer

Recognize Story Structure

Plot

Lesson 11 ▶

Sid Scores
Land of Ice
My Father's Feet

Make Inferences

Words with _or_ and _ore_

Lesson 12 ▶

Fox and His Big Wish
King Midas and His Gold
Gold and Money

Ask Questions

Setting

13

Big Idea

Authors use characters to tell a story.

Enduring ! Understanding

Characters in stories are alike in some ways and different in other ways.

Essential ? Question

How can readers tell if characters are alike or different?

Spelling Words

Words with Short Vowel *e*

set	get
sent	all
ten	call
tell	make
let	of

Fluency

Expression

Phonics

Words with /e/ *e*

Comprehension

Compare and Contrast

Answer Questions

Robust Vocabulary

Listening and Speaking Words

chorus

odor

shoved

assemble

consume

enthusiastic

Words to Know

High-Frequency Words

day

eat

first

said

time

was

Writing

• Sentences About Events

• Ideas

Lesson 7

1 Get Started Story

Ten Eggs

by Nancy Furstinger • illustrated by Lori Lohstoeter

2 Genre: Fantasy

Little Red Hen Gets Help

by Kenneth Spengler
illustrated by Margaret Spengler

Let's Make Tortillas!

3 Genre: Recipe

Ten Eggs

by Nancy Furstinger

illustrated
by Lori Lohstoeter

16

Ten hens had ten eggs.

Jen got six eggs.
Ken got the rest.

Jen mixed the eggs.
Ken mixed the eggs.

What a big mess!

Did Jen and Ken get help?

Yes! Mom got a pan.
In went the eggs.

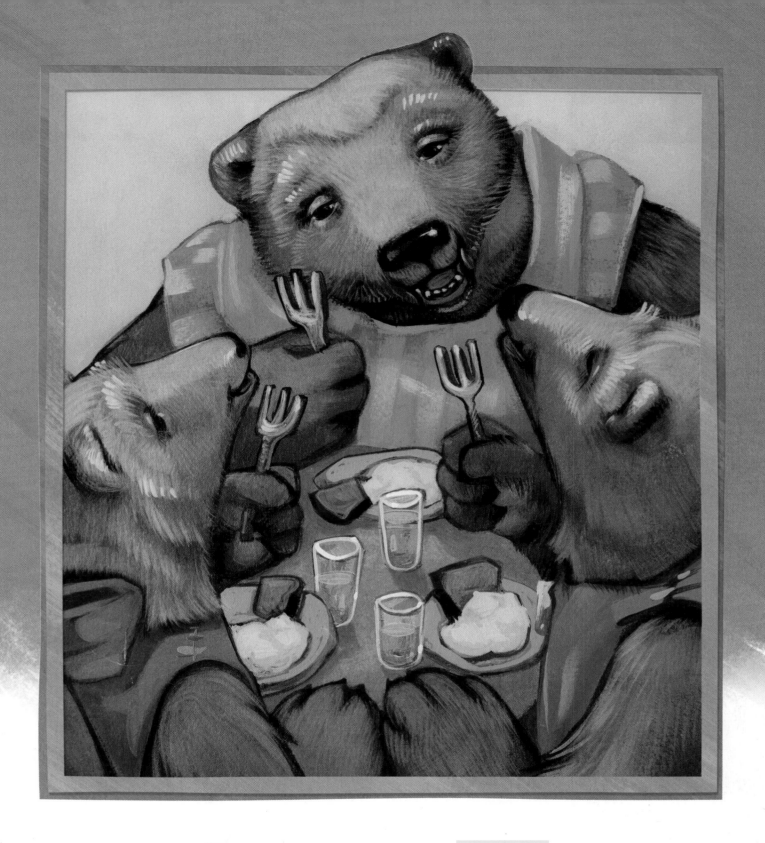

What did Mom make?
The best eggs yet!

Phonics Skill

Short Vowel <u>e</u>

The letter **<u>e</u>** can stand for the sound at the beginning of the words **<u>egg</u>** and **<u>elephant</u>**.

egg   **elephant**

The letter **<u>e</u>** can stand for the sound in the middle of the words **<u>pen</u>** and **<u>net</u>**.

pen   **net**

**Look at each picture. Read the words.
Tell which word names the picture.**

ten

hen

him

vent

vat

vest

 www.harcourtschool.com/storytown

Try This!

Read the sentences.

I have a pet.

He is called Jet.

He went to the vet.

Now he can rest.

Words to Know

day

said

eat

first

time

was

26

"It is a hot **day**," **said** Hen.

"Let's **eat**," said Cat.

"**First** add some of this," said Fox.

"Now it is **time** to add this," said Pig.

"That **was** fast!" said Hen.

Little Red Hen
Gets Help
by Kenneth Spengler
illustrated by Margaret Spengler

Fantasy

Genre Study

A **fantasy** is a made-up story. The events could never really happen.

What Little Red Hen Asks	What the Characters Say and Do

Comprehension Strategy

Answer Questions To answer questions about the story, think about the words you read. Use what you already know to figure out answers, too.

Little Red Hen Gets Help

by Kenneth Spengler

illustrated by Margaret Spengler

One day, Little Red Hen got up.
She was hungry.

"Who wants to eat this?" she asked.

"Not I," said Cat.

"I can't," said Fox.

"Oh, no," said Pig.

"Who wants tacos?" asked Red Hen.

"I do!" they all yelled.

"Will you help make some tacos?"

"Yes!" said Cat.
"I will!" said Fox.
"Let me, too!" said Pig.

Red Hen fed Cat, Fox, and Pig.

"What a mess! Who will pick up?"

"Not I," said Cat.

"I can't," said Fox.

"Oh, no," said Pig.

"We will help!" called the ants.

"Thank you, ants" said Red Hen.
"Next time, I will ask you first!"

Think Critically

1 How are the ants like Cat, Pig, and Fox? How are they different? COMPARE AND CONTRAST

2 What happens to the kitchen when Cat, Pig, and Fox make tacos? DETAILS

3 Why does Little Red Hen need help cleaning? MAKE INFERENCES

4 Why does Little Red Hen say she will ask the ants first to help? DRAW CONCLUSIONS

5 **WRITE** Write about a time when someone helped you. WRITING RESPONSE

Meet the Author
Kenneth Spengler

Kenneth Spengler likes to write funny stories.
He worked with his wife, Margaret, on this one.

"I liked writing this story because I love food,
especially tacos! Just like the Little Red Hen, I like
help when I cook. Sometimes we spill food on the
floor. Our dog, Jackie, helps clean it up, though,
not ants!"

Meet the Illustrator
Margaret Spengler

Margaret Spengler is the artist who made the pictures for this story. She painted them on sand paper with pastel chalk and water. The thing she likes best about being an artist is being creative.

66I like the Little Red Hen because she is smart and caring. I also like the way she shares with her friends.99

Recipe

Let's Make Tortillas!

1½ cups flour

½ teaspoon salt

2 tablespoons oil

½ cup warm water

1 Mix the flour, salt, oil, and water.

2 Roll six balls.
Make six circles.

3 Cook in a pan.

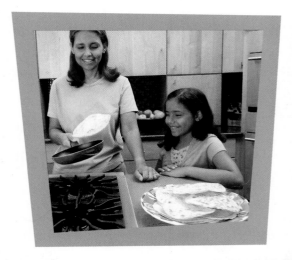

4 Eat the tortillas!
You can fill them
to make tacos.

Connections

Comparing Texts

1. What did you find out about making tacos from the story? What did you learn from the recipe?

2. How do you help clean up at home?

3. Which of Little Red Hen's jobs would you do best? Tell why.

Writing

Imagine that you are in the story. Write about how you would help.

What Little Red Hen Asks	How I Would Help

Phonics

Make and read new words.

Start with **egg**.

Add $\boxed{\text{l}}$ in front of $\boxed{\text{e}}$. Take off $\boxed{\text{g}}$.

Change $\boxed{\text{g}}$ to $\boxed{\text{t}}$.

Change $\boxed{\text{l}}$ to $\boxed{\text{w}}$.

Add $\boxed{\text{n}}$ after $\boxed{\text{e}}$.

Fluency Practice

Work with a small group. Decide who will be each animal in "Little Red Hen Gets Help." Read the story. Use your voice to show how your character feels. Look at the end marks of sentences to help you.

I will!

Yes!

Let me, too!

Reading-Writing Connection

Describing an Event

"Little Red Hen Gets Help" is about something that Little Red Hen and her friends did. After we read the story, we wrote about something that we did.

▶ **First, we talked about the story.**

▶ **Next, we talked about things we have done. We made up sentences to tell about an event.**

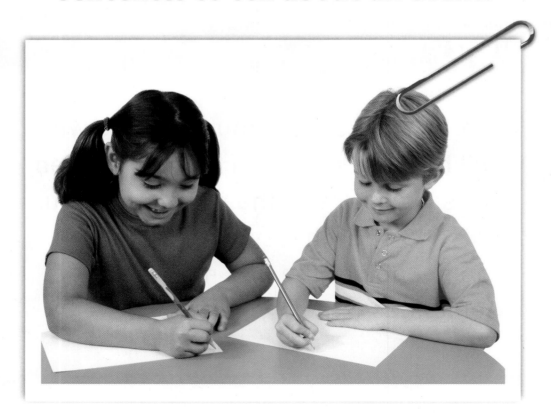

▶ **Last, we read our sentences.**

Our class went to
the zoo. We saw lions,
bears, and many other
animals. We ate lunch
at the zoo, and then
we came home. We all
had a great time!

GPS Focus Wall

Big 💡 Idea
Readers use details in stories to "see" the story.

Enduring ❗ Understanding
Details are small bits of information that help the reader learn more about something in the story.

Essential ❓ Question
How do details in a story help readers see something in their mind?

Spelling Words

Words with *th*

then	with
them	ten
this	get
that	said
path	was

Fluency

Expression

Phonics

Words with /th/ *th*

th

Comprehension

Details

Use Graphic Organizers

Words to Know

High-Frequency Words

- don't
- her
- line
- Mr.
- new
- says
- water

Writing

- Questions
- Conventions

Robust Vocabulary

Listening and Speaking Words

- applauded
- chatty
- gather
- duty
- envy
- resent

Lesson 8

1 Get Started **Story**

Thanks, Seth!

by Anne Mansk ◆ illustrated by Linda Bronson

2 Genre: Realistic Fiction

Beth's Job

by Carole Roberts
Illustrated by Michael Garland

Flowers Grow

3 Genre: Nonfiction

Thanks, Seth!

by Anne Mansk
illustrated by Linda Bronson

54

Ben is not glad.
"Can I do this math?"

Seth sees Ben.
"I can help Ben," thinks Seth.

Ben sees Seth.
Seth tells Ben he can help.

Seth helps Ben with the task.

Now Ben can add fast.

Seth and Ben are glad!
Ben did all the math.

Thanks, Seth!

Focus Skill

 Details

Details give small bits of information about something. Details help you picture the person, animal, place, or thing in your mind.

Look at the picture.

It shows details of what this child is having for lunch.

Tell about this picture. What details do you see?

 Try This!

Look at the picture. Tell how the details help you understand what is happening.

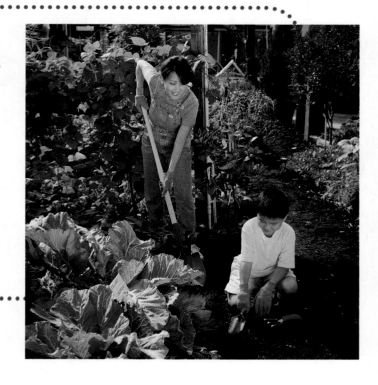

www.harcourtschool.com/storytown

Words to Know

don't

says

water

Mr.

new

line

her

64

"I **don't** have a job," **says** Beth.

"You can **water** this plant," **Mr.** Hall says.

Max has a **new** job, too.

He helps Hops.

We get in **line** to pet **her**.

GO online www.harcourtschool.com/storytown

Beth's Job

by Carole Roberts
illustrated by Michael Garland

Realistic Fiction

Genre Study

Realistic fiction stories are made up, but they could happen in real life.

Beginning

↓

Middle

↓

Ending

Comprehension Strategy

Use Graphic Organizers
A story map can help you understand and remember the beginning, middle, and ending of a story.

Beth's Job

by Carole Roberts
illustrated by Michael Garland

It's the day for new jobs.

Class Jobs
Max - pet
Beth - plant
Ann - eggs
Jeff - line
Glen - flag
Jill - clock

Monday

"What is my job?" asks Beth.

"You can water the plant,"
says Mr. Hall.

"Oh, no," thinks Beth.

Max helps with Hops.
Hops is the class pet.

"I want that job," thinks Beth.

Ann helps with the eggs.

Beth wants that job.

Jeff is first in line.

Beth wants that job, too.

Glen gets to hold the flag.

"I want to hold the flag,"
thinks Beth.

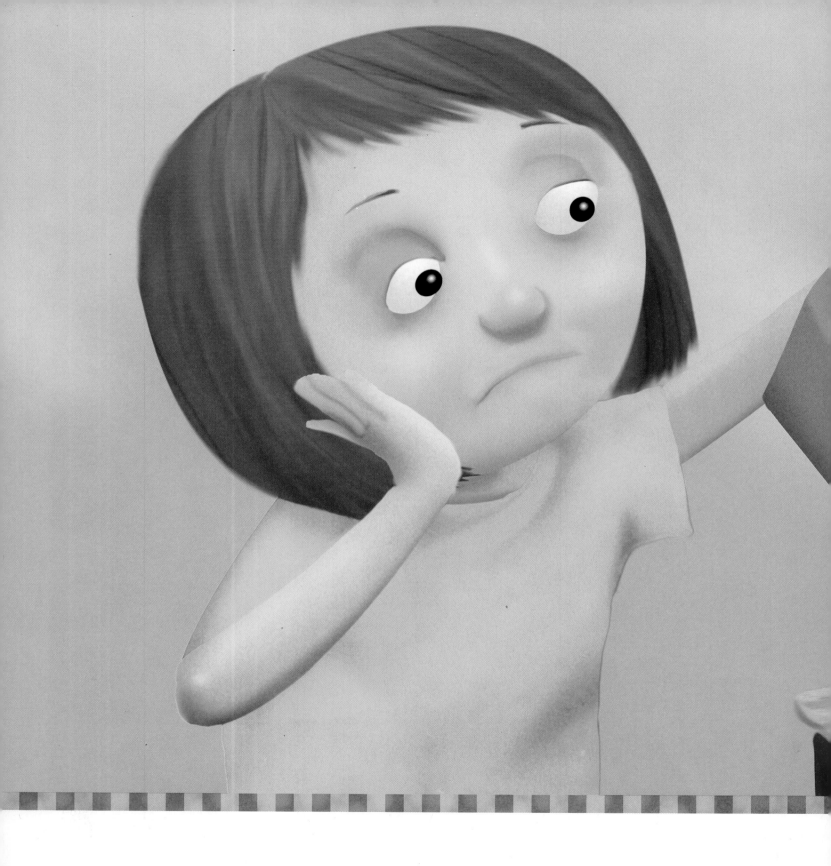

"I don't like this plant," thinks Beth.

"I want a new job."

"Look at this flower, Beth!"
says Mr. Hall.

"Oh, my!" says the class.

"Oh, my!" says Beth.
"How did that get there?"

"This job is the best!"
Beth likes her job at last!

Think Critically

1 How does Beth feel about her job when the story begins? How does she feel at the end? Why?

COMPARE AND CONTRAST

2 What is one thing Beth does to help the plant? DETAILS

3 Why do you think Beth wants to help with the eggs? MAKE INFERENCES

4 How does Beth's job make the classroom a better place?

DRAW CONCLUSIONS

5 **WRITE** Write about a job you enjoy doing. Tell why that job is important. WRITING RESPONSE

Meet the Illustrator
Michael Garland

Michael Garland has written and illustrated many books for children. He spent his childhood in New York exploring the woods, playing sports, and drawing. Drawing was the thing he did best. When he would draw something in school, his teachers would often show it to the class and put it up on the bulletin board. This helped him to decide he wanted to become an artist.

GO online www.harcourtschool.com/storytown

Flowers Grow

Nonfiction

Flowers Grow

A plant needs water, light, air, and soil to grow.

seed

seedling

young plant

bud

flower

The plant grows.

Now there is a flower.
How nice!

Connections

Comparing Texts

1. How is the plant in "Beth's Job" like the one in "Flowers Grow"?

2. How is Beth's classroom like your classroom? How is it different?

3. Tell about a job you have had at school.

Writing

Draw three pictures to show how Beth feels at the beginning, middle, and end of the story. Label each picture with a word or sentence.

Beth is sad because she doesn't like her job.

Phonics

Make and read new words.

Start with **path**.

Take away **pa**. Add **in** after **th**.

Change **i** to **a** .

Add **k** to the end.

Fluency Practice

Read the story aloud with a small group. Look at the end marks of the sentences as you read. Use your voice to show how Beth and her classmates feel.

Big Idea
The details used in a selection describe things for the reader.

Enduring ! Understanding
Details help the reader answer questions about things in the selection.

Essential ? Question
How do details help the reader understand a selection?

Spelling Words
Words with Short Vowel *u*

us	club
bus	with
must	then
cut	don't
cub	says

Fluency
Phrasing

Phonics
Words with /u/ *u*

Uu

u

Comprehension
 Details

 Monitor Comprehension: Adjust Reading Rate

Robust Vocabulary
Listening and Speaking Words
- claimed
- dine
- groaned
- classify
- function
- nutritious

Words to Know
High-Frequency Words
- be
- does
- food
- grow
- live
- many

Writing
- Lists
- Organization

Lesson 9

1 Get Started Story

A Nut Falls
by Sandra Widener
illustrated by Doug Bowles

2 Genre: Nonfiction

Plants Can't Jump
by Ned Crowley

Cornfield Leaves
by Lessie Jones Little
illustrated by Don Tate

3 Genre: Poetry

Phonics
Words with short vowel <u>u</u>

Words to Know

Review

now

tree

A Nut Falls

by Sandra Widener

illustrated by
Doug Bowles

Thud! A nut falls in mud.

Sun falls on that nut.
Next that nut gets wet.

The stem pops up!
That nut is now a small plant.

The plant is tall.
It is a big nut tree!

Small buds are on that tree.
Small nuts are on that tree.

Small nuts get big.
Men pick nuts off the tree.

A nut fell in mud.
That nut is now a big tree!

Focus Skill

Details

Details give small bits of information about something. Details can tell what something looks like, how it sounds, or what it does.

Look at the picture.

The artist is drawing details he sees in the real flower.

Tell about this picture. What details do you see?

Look closely at the picture. Think about the details you see. Tell what you think this machine does.

Words to Know

High-Frequency Words

live

does

grow

many

be

food

Where can a plant **live**?

Where **does** it **grow**?

Many plants can **be food**.

Many can grow flowers.

 www.harcourtschool.com/storytown

105

Nonfiction

Genre Study

A **nonfiction** selection tells about things that are real and often has photographs.

K What I Know	W What I Want to Know	L What I Learned

Comprehension Strategy

Monitor Comprehension: Reading Rate Read along smoothly with the rhythm and rhyme of this nonfiction poem. Slow down to read important information.

Plants Can't Jump

by Ned Crowley

Plants can't jump!
Plants can't hop.

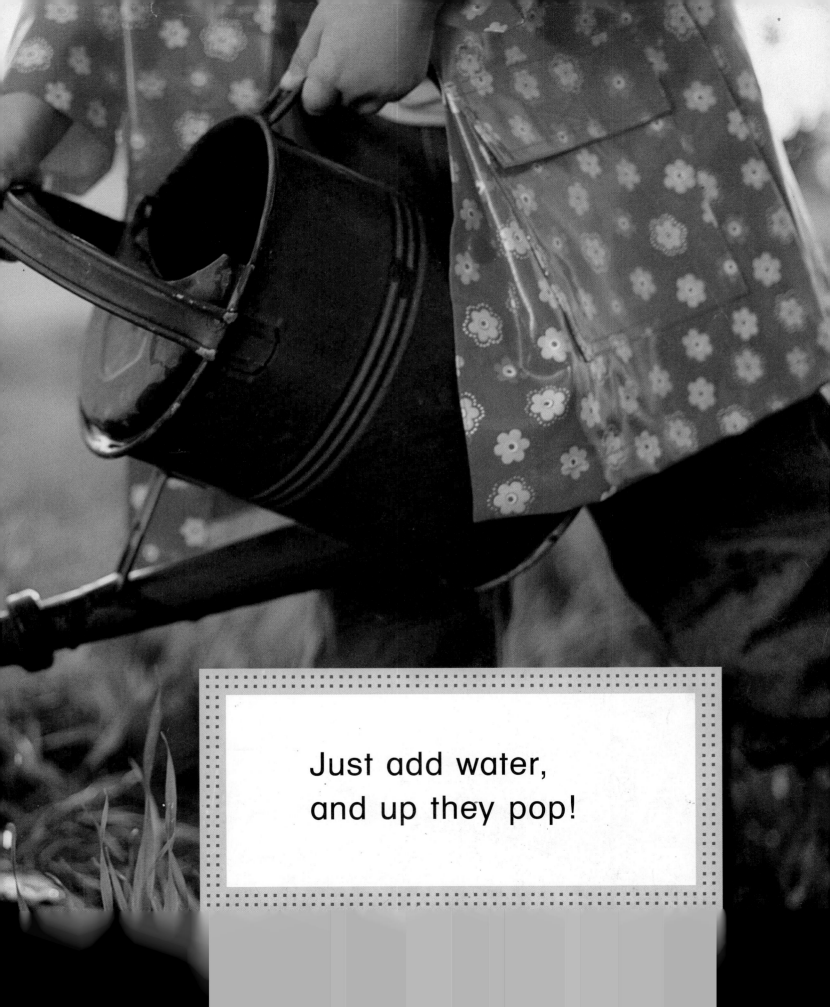

Just add water,
and up they pop!

Roots grow down.
Stems grow up.

Plants can look like
bells and cups.

Plants have spots
and dots and bumps.

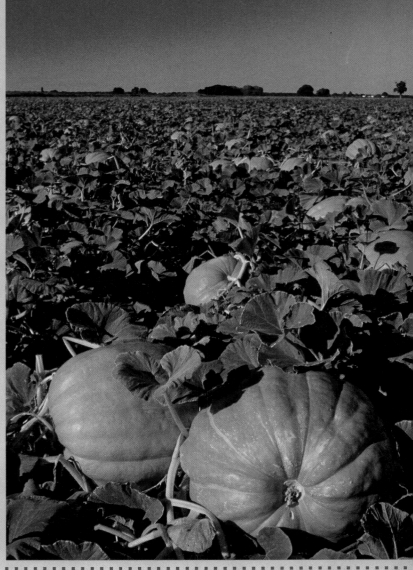

Plants can be thin.
Plants can be plump.

A plant has leaves,
but what do they give?

Leaves make food
so a plant can live.

Plants must get water.
It helps them grow.

Plip, plop, plip!
Where does it go?

Plants live in sand.
Plants live in mud.

This plant has flowers.
That one has a bud.

If some bugs want food,
they eat plants.

Some plants eat bugs
like moths and ants!

Plants are red
and pink and black.

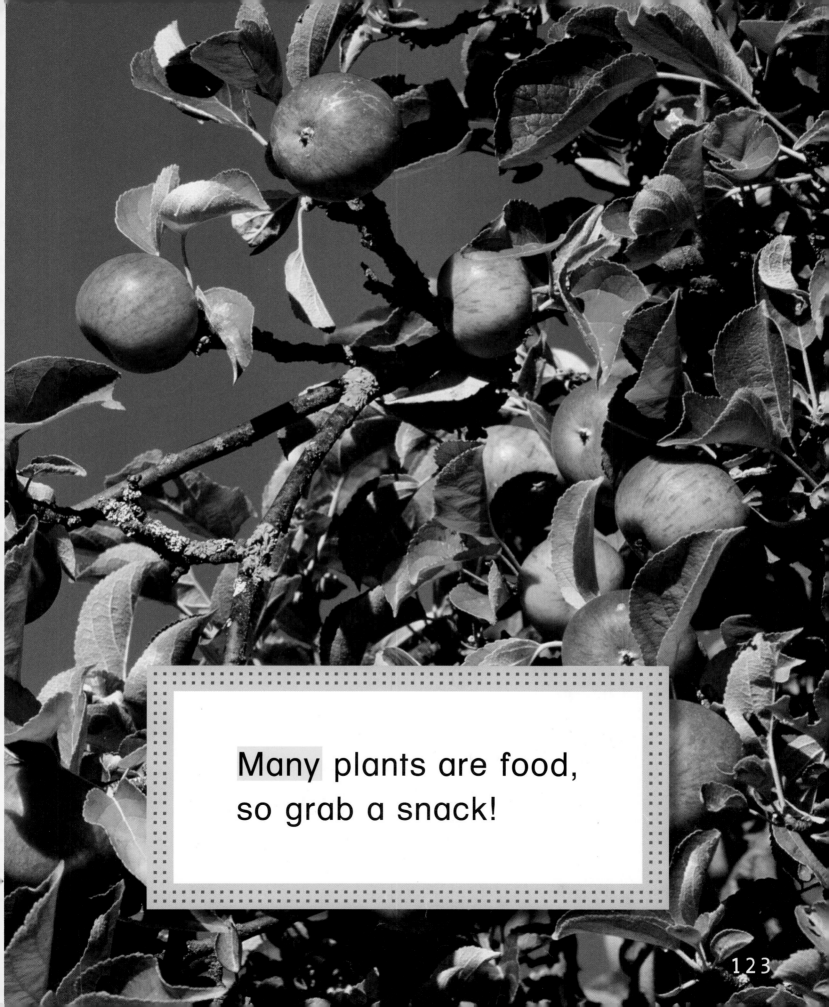

Many plants are food,
so grab a snack!

Plants can't jump,
but they don't fuss.

Plants can grow,
just like us!

Think Critically

1 What do leaves do for plants?

DRAW CONCLUSIONS

2 What do a plant's roots do? What does the stem do? DETAILS

3 What are different ways a plant can get water? DRAW CONCLUSIONS

4 Why do you think some plants eat bugs? MAKE INFERENCES

5 **WRITE** Which do you like better—a plant with flowers or a plant you can eat? Tell why. WRITING RESPONSE

Meet the Author
Ned Crowley

Ned Crowley is a writer and illustrator.
Recently, he has been writing books
about bugs and plants. Mr. Crowley
says books like these are fun to write.
When he looks at pictures of plants or
bugs, he tries to give them personalities
just like people.

Mr. Crowley has three daughters. He
says that they like plants a lot more
than bugs!

 www.harcourtschool.com/storytown

Cornfield
Leaves

by Lessie Jones Little
Illustrated by Don Tate

Poetry

Teacher Read-Aloud

Cornfield Leaves

by Lessie Jones Little
illustrated by Don Tate

Silky ribbons long and green,
Dotted with sparkling dew,
Waving in the summer breeze
Under a roof of blue.

Keep on waving in the breeze,
Keep on sparkling, too,
And every time you wave at me,
I'll wave right back at you.

Connections

Comparing Texts

1 How are "Plants Can't Jump" and the poem "Cornfield Leaves" alike?

2 Tell about an interesting plant you have seen at home or at school.

3 What is your favorite food that comes from a plant?

Writing

Draw a picture of your favorite plant. Label the parts of your plant. Write about why you like it.

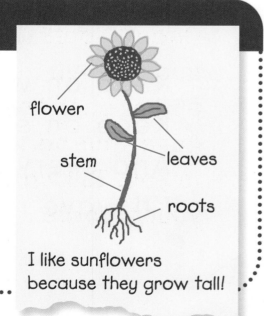

flower

stem

leaves

roots

I like sunflowers because they grow tall!

Phonics

Make and read new words.

Start with **us**.

Add $\boxed{b}$ at the beginning.

Change $\boxed{s}$ to $\boxed{d}$.

Change $\boxed{b}$ to $\boxed{m}$.

Change $\boxed{d}$ to $\boxed{s}$ $\boxed{t}$.

Fluency Practice

Read "Plants Can't Jump" to a partner. Pause at the end of each line. Then have your partner read it to you. Tell which part is your favorite.

Plants can't jump!
Plants can't hop.

Just add water, and up they pop!

Big Idea

A story's plot can teach readers lessons about themselves and their friends.

Enduring ! Understanding

The plot in a story has a beginning, middle, and ending.

Essential ? Question

How is real life like the plot of a story?

Spelling Words

Words with *ng*

long	thing
song	us
sing	must
ring	does
bring	food

Fluency

Phrasing

Phonics

Words with /ng/*ng*

ng

Comprehension

 Plot

 Recognize Story Structure

Words to Know

High-Frequency Words

- arms
- every
- feet
- head
- school
- use
- way
- your

Writing

- Dialogue
- Voice

Robust Vocabulary

Listening and Speaking Words

- ashamed
- mused
- soared
- athletic
- awkward
- superb

Lesson 10

1 Get Started **Story**

Frog Gets His Song

by Linda Barr   illustrated by Jui Ishida

2 Genre: Realistic Fiction

Soccer Song

by Patricia Reilly Giff
illustrated by
Blanche Sims

Now You Know About

Soccer

3 Genre: Nonfiction

Frog Gets His Song
by Linda Barr illustrated by Jui Ishida

Phonics
Words with <u>ng</u>

Words to Know

Review

her

be

said

Frog Gets His Song

by Linda Barr

illustrated by Jui Ishida

134

Ming had Frog in her grip.
Ming looked at him with a big grin.

Frog looked at Ming's long
fangs. "Help!" yelled Frog.
"Let me go!"

"Be still!" Ming hissed. "Sing me a song and I will let you go."

"Sing?" grunted Frog. "Frogs can't sing!"

"Do frogs have lungs?" Ming asked.

"Yes," Frog said.

"Then sing!" Ming snapped.

Frog filled his lungs and sang.
His song rang out. Frog sang
and sang and sang.

Did Ming let Frog go? Yes.
Did Frog stop singing? No!

Frogs are still singing!

Focus Skill

 Plot

The events that make up a story are called
the **plot**. The **plot** of a story is what happens
in that story.

Look at the pictures.

These pictures show a story. The plot is
about children finding a lost dog.

The pictures show events in a story.
What is the plot?

Try This!

Look at the picture. Choose the words that name the plot of a story about these people.

- enjoying winter activities

- playing with pets

- having a picnic

GO online www.harcourtschool.com/storytown

143

Words to Know

High-Frequency Words

school

every

your

feet

use

arms

head

way

144

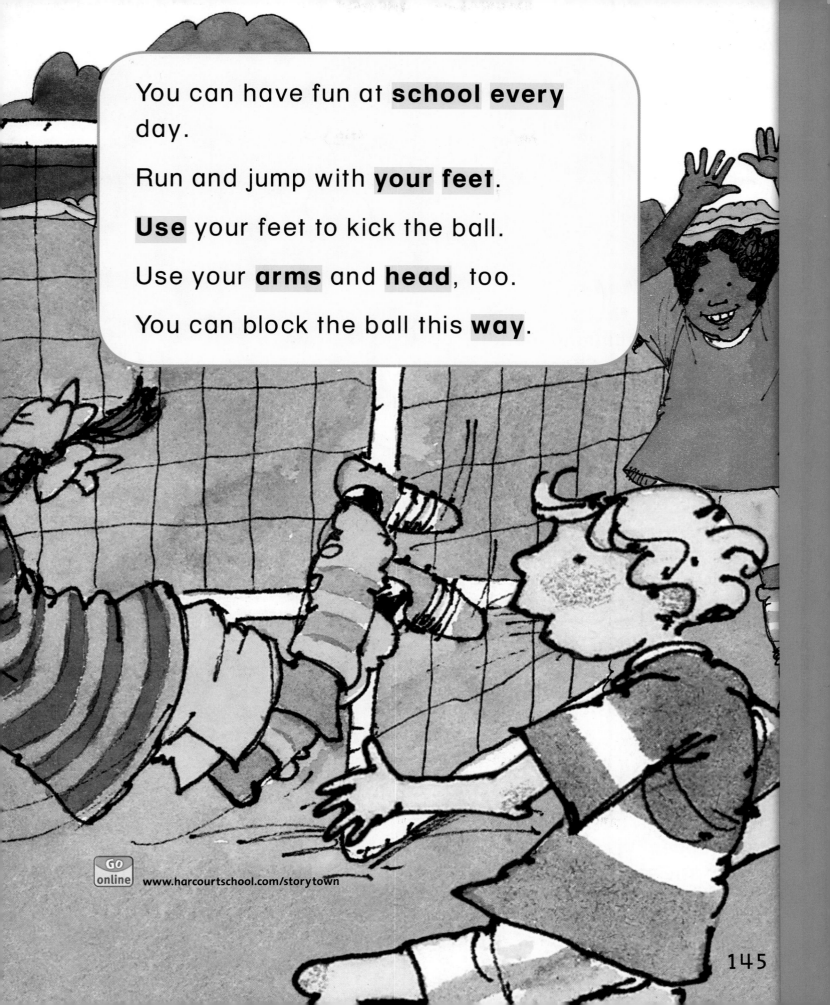

You can have fun at **school every** day.

Run and jump with **your feet**.

Use your feet to kick the ball.

Use your **arms** and **head**, too.

You can block the ball this **way**.

Realistic Fiction

Genre Study
Realistic fiction stories have a beginning, middle, and ending. Characters do things that could happen in real life.

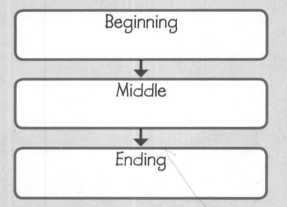

Beginning

↓

Middle

↓

Ending

Comprehension Strategy
Recognize Story Structure As you read, think about what is happening in each part of the story.

Meow

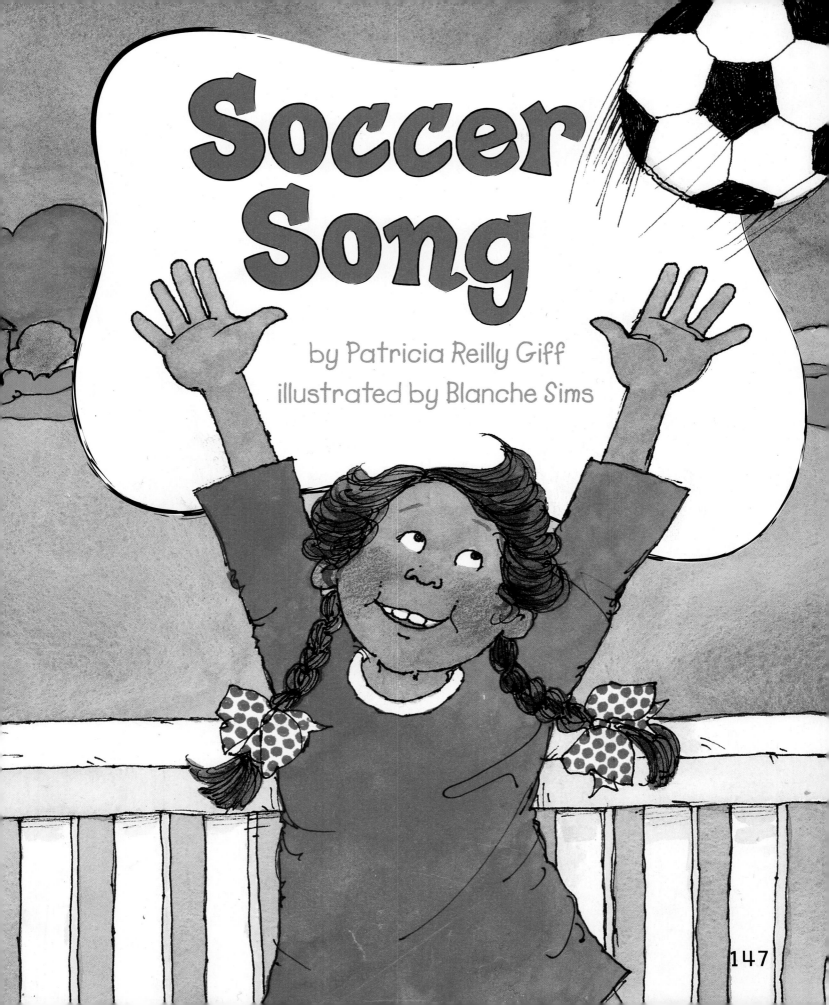

Soccer Song

by Patricia Reilly Giff

illustrated by Blanche Sims

Jill had long arms.
She had strong hands.

One day, Jill got Gus.
"Jill did it!" called Tom.
"Meow," said Gus.

One day, Fran swung the bat.
Her ball went up.
Jill jumped up.

Meow

"Jill got it!" yelled the kids.
"Meow," said Gus.

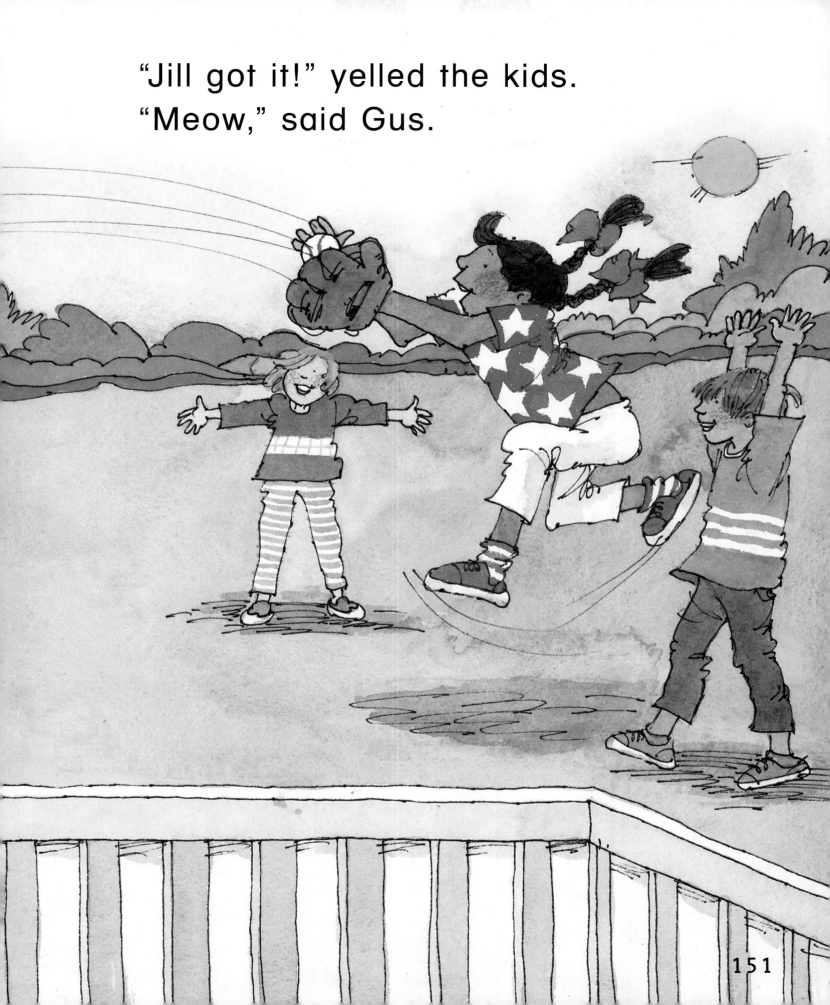

At school, Miss King said,
"It's soccer time! Kick the
ball with your feet."

"Don't use your hands!"
said Tom.

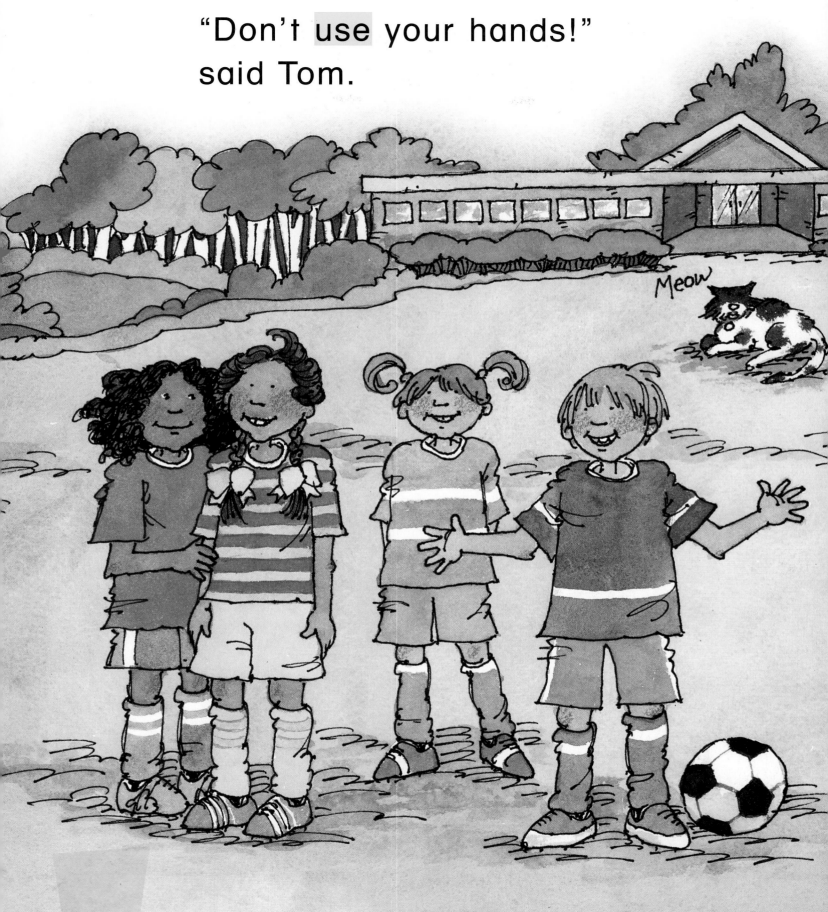

Jill's legs went this way.
The ball went that way.

Jill's head went this way.
The ball went that way.

Jill hung her head.

"You have strong arms and hands," said Tom. "You got Gus out of a tree."

"You got my ball, too," said Fran.

"A goalie can use her hands," said Miss King.

The next day, Jill was goalie. She
used her strong arms and hands.
She blocked the ball every time.

"You did it!" yelled Tom and Fran.

"Jump, block! I am strong!
This is my soccer song!" sang Jill.
"Meow!" sang Gus.

Think Critically

1 Why does Jill have trouble learning to play soccer at first? PLOT

2 What are some things that Jill can do well? DETAILS

3 Why is Jill a good goalie? DRAW CONCLUSIONS

4 Do you think Jill will keep playing soccer? Tell why or why not. MAKE INFERENCES

5 **WRITE** Write about something you can do well. WRITING RESPONSE

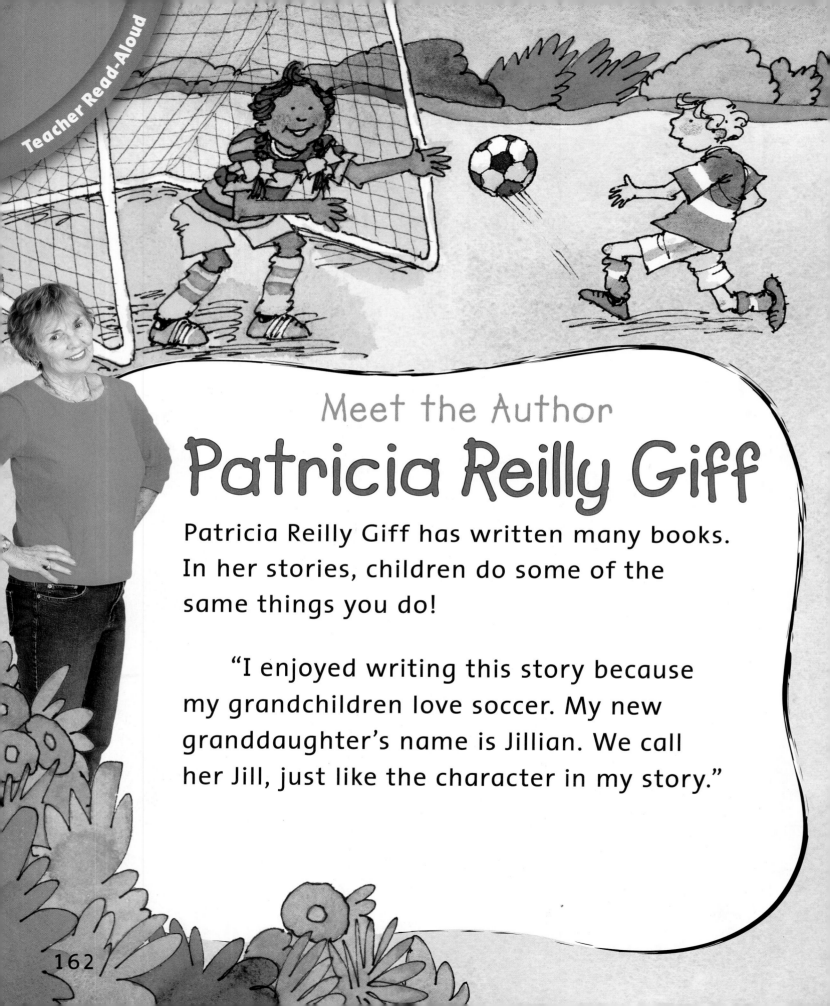

Meet the Author

Patricia Reilly Giff

Patricia Reilly Giff has written many books. In her stories, children do some of the same things you do!

"I enjoyed writing this story because my grandchildren love soccer. My new granddaughter's name is Jillian. We call her Jill, just like the character in my story."

Meet the Illustrator
Blanche Sims

Blanche Sims has illustrated many children's books. She says that the best part about being an artist is drawing. She has always loved to draw! When Blanche Sims was in school, one of her teachers even hung up a huge piece of paper in the classroom for her to fill with her artwork.

Meow

Now You
Know About
Soccer

Nonfiction

Now You Know About Soccer

People all over the world play soccer. Soccer players wear special clothes.

shirt

shorts

socks

soccer ball

shin guards

cleats

Teams must practice. It's fun!

A team gets the ball in the other team's goal. One point!

Teams show they are good sports. "Good game!" they say.

Connections

Comparing Texts

1 What did you learn about soccer from the story? What more did you learn from the article?

2 What games and sports have you played at school or at home?

3 What is your favorite game or sport? Why?

Writing

Draw a picture of yourself learning to play a game or sport. Write what happened. Write some of the words you said.

I learned to play Tee Ball.
I had to practice a lot.
Now I can hit the ball.
It's fun!

Run!

I hit it!

Make and read new words.

Start with **long**.

Change **l** to **s**.

Add **t** **r** after **s**.

Change **o** to **i**.

Take out **r**.

Fluency Practice

Read with a partner. Take turns reading pages of the story. Make it sound as if the characters are really talking. Remember to pause a little at commas and end marks.

Big 💡 Idea

Nonfiction selections use facts to show readers how things are alike or different.

Enduring ❗ Understanding

Good readers use clue words such as *like*, *both*, and *same* to see how things are alike in nonfiction selections.

Essential ❓ Question

How do readers use word clues to look for the way things are alike?

Spelling Words

Words with *or* and *ore*

or	sort
for	long
form	bring
more	your
store	head

Fluency

Phrasing

Phonics

Words with /ôr/ *or*, *ore*

or
ore

Comprehension

 Compare and Contrast

 Monitor Comprehension: Make Inferences

Words to Know

High-Frequency Words

animals
cold
fish
from
their
under
very

Writing

• Interview Questions
• Organization

Robust Vocabulary

Listening and Speaking Words

nuzzled
pranced
raging
adapt
intriguing
inhabit

Lesson 11

1 Get Started Story

Sid Scores
by Deanne W. Kells   illustrated by Pierre Pratt

2 Genre: Nonfiction

Land of Ice
by Norbert Wu

My Father's Feet
by Judy Sierra

3 Genre: Poetry

Phonics
Words with <u>or</u>

Words to Know

Review

lives

was

now

Sid Scores

by Deanne W. Kells

illustrated by Pierre Pratt

Sid lives in the North.
He likes all sports.

Sid was born to win.
Sid scores and scores.
Win, Sid, win!

Sid can swim more than six laps.
He has good form.

Sid can do more.
He can jump past the cord.

Sid can flip and flop.
He can skim and skid.
More, Sid, more!

Sid is sore and worn out.
He will rest now.

Sid will snort and snore.
Sid will score more in the morning.

Phonics Skill

Words with or and ore

The letters **or** and **ore** can stand for the sound at the beginning of **orange**, in the middle of **fork**, and at the end of **store**.

orange

fork

store

Look at each picture. Read the words. Which word tells about the picture?

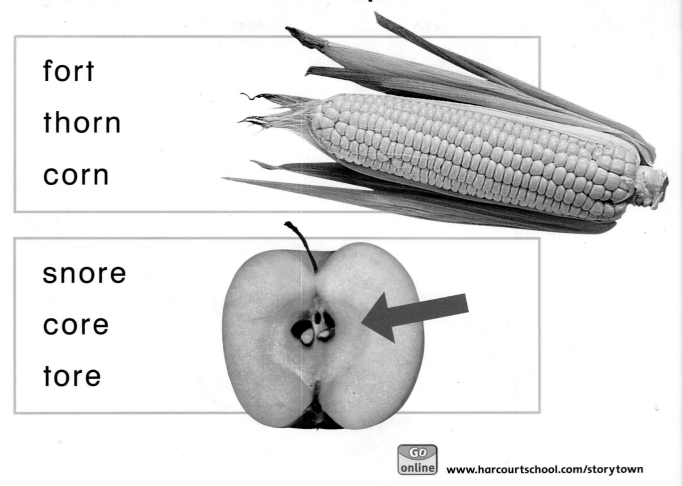

fort

thorn

corn

snore

core

tore

 www.harcourtschool.com/storytown

Try This!

Read the sentences.

We went to the store for food. My mom got some corn. My dad got more eggs. I got a new hat and wore it home.

Words to Know

High-Frequency Words

very

cold

fish

their

from

animals

under

It is **very cold**. Many **fish** live here. Fish use **their** fins to swim. What does this fish eat? Big fish can eat small fish or get food **from** plants.

More **animals** live here. Many of them can swim **under** the water, too.

GO online www.harcourtschool.com/storytown

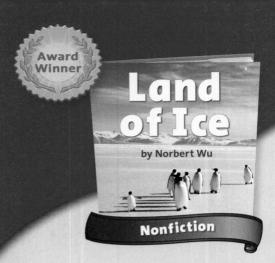

Land of Ice
by Norbert Wu

Nonfiction

Genre Study

A **nonfiction** selection gives many facts about real things and often has photographs.

Comprehension Strategy

Monitor Comprehension: Make Inferences Think about what the words say and what you already know to figure out what the selection is about.

Land of Ice

by Norbert Wu

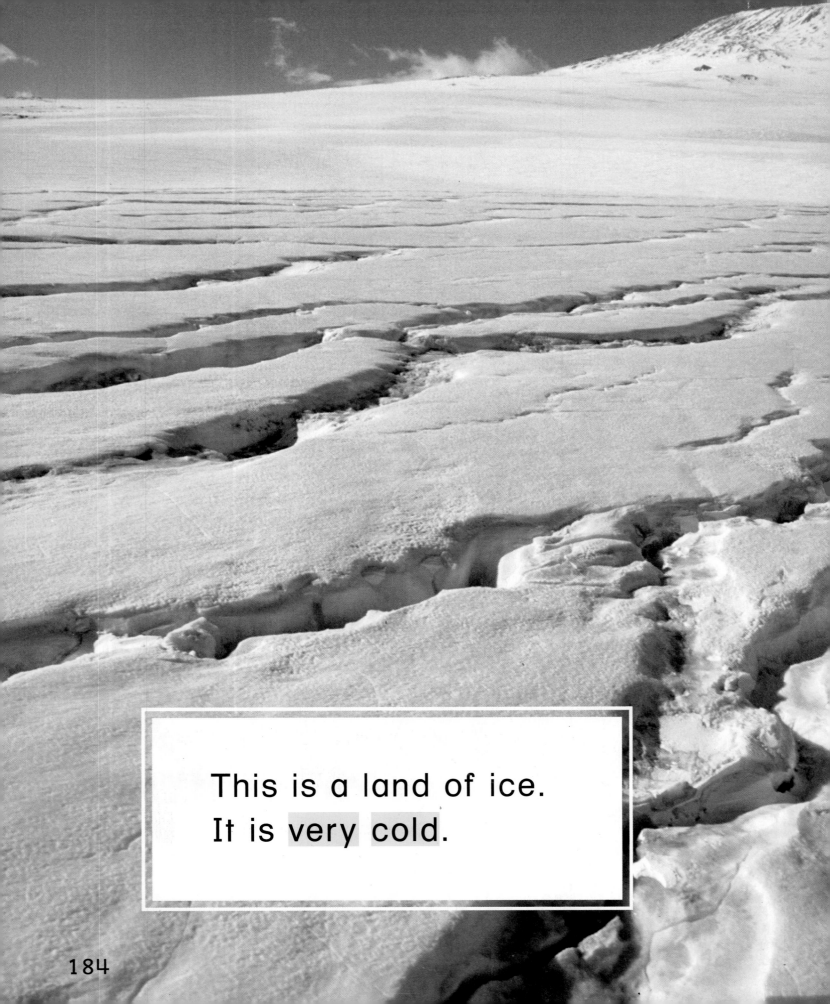

This is a land of ice.
It is very cold.

What is out here?
Can things live in
this land?

Look! This is a seal with a
small pup that was just born.
How can seals live here?

Seals have lots of fat and thick fur. This makes them snug.

Here is a small penguin.

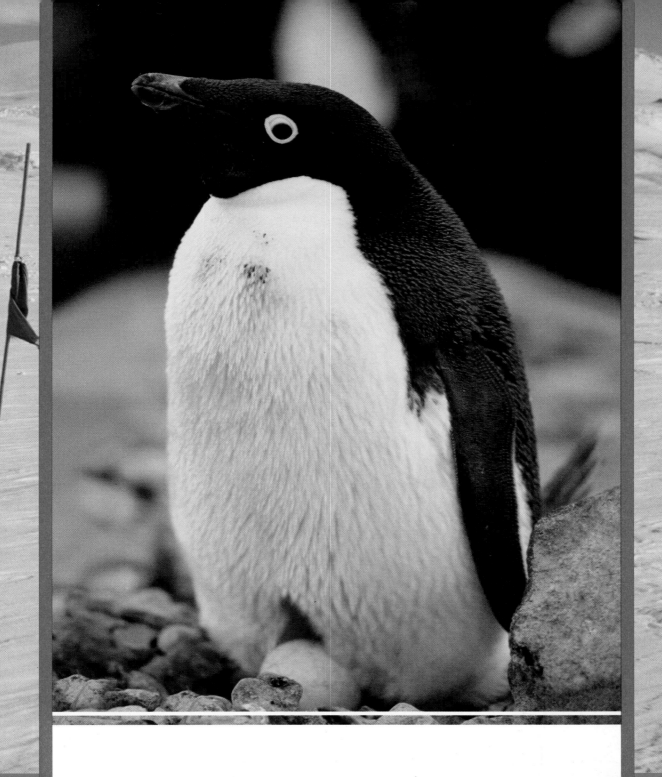

This sort of penguin makes
nests on rocks and cliffs.
Penguins come from eggs.

Do more things live here?
Let's go under the ice.

It's beautiful! You can still
see the sun.

You can see red sea stars.

There are animals that look like plants!

You can see an
octopus, too.

This animal has long strings that sting small animals. This helps it get its food.

This small fish likes ice. It does not get too cold. It has a nest of eggs in the ice.

This mom is helping her little one swim in the cold water.

Here are some more penguins.
Look at them go!

They use their wings to swim
very fast. Flap, flap, flap!
Where will they go next?

This IS a land of ice...
and much more!

Think Critically

1 How is the land different from what is under the water? How is it the same? COMPARE AND CONTRAST

2 What are some animals that live in the land of ice? DETAILS

3 Why do you think penguins like to live there? DRAW CONCLUSIONS

4 Does it look as if people could live there? Why or why not? MAKE INFERENCES

5 **WRITE** Write about the most interesting animal in "Land of Ice."

WRITING RESPONSE

Meet the Author/Photographer
Norbert Wu

Norbert Wu likes to take pictures in unusual places, like under the ice in Antarctica! He has seen many animals there, including lots of penguins. He says that penguins walk oddly on land, but are at home in the water. They swim around fast, just like little jet planes!

"I wrote this story because I want you to know that our world is a beautiful and fragile place."

GO online www.harcourtschool.com/storytown

My
Father's
Feet

by Judy Sierra

Poetry

My Father's Feet

by Judy Sierra

To keep myself up off the ice,
I find my father's feet are nice.
I snuggle in his belly fluff,
And that's how I stay warm enough.

But when my father takes a walk,
My cozy world begins to rock.
He shuffles left, I hold on tight.
Oh no! He's wobbling to the right.

Not left again! Oops, here he goes.
Do you suppose my father knows
I'm hanging on to his warm toes?

Connections

Comparing Texts

1. Would the penguins from the poem like the land of ice? Tell why or why not.

2. How is the place in "Land of Ice" like where you live? How is it different?

3. What would you do in the land of ice?

Writing

Write sentences about "Land of Ice." Tell what you would see, hear, smell, taste, and feel if you were there.

> The land of ice is very cold. There is snow and ice all around.

206

Phonics

Make and read new words.

Start with **<u>for</u>**.

Add **t** at the end.

Change **f** to **s**.

Change **t** to **e**.

Change **s** to **m**.

Fluency Practice

Read a favorite part of the story or poem to a partner. Stop a little at end marks and commas to help you read one "chunk" at a time.

GPS Focus Wall

Big Idea
Stories are written about real and make-believe times and places.

Enduring ! Understanding
Words and other clues point readers to when and where the story takes place.

Essential ? Question
How do word clues help the reader understand where and when the story takes place?

Spelling Words

Words with *sh*

shop	fish
shot	for
shut	more
rush	from
wish	very

Fluency

Expression

Phonics

Words with /sh/*sh*

sh

Comprehension

 Setting

 Ask Questions

Robust Vocabulary

Listening and Speaking Words

reward

handsomely

cruel

greedy

consequences

regret

Words to Know

High-Frequency Words

came

could

gold

happy

made

night

saw

were

Writing

• Riddles
• Conventions

Lesson 12

1 Get Started Story

Fox and His Big Wish

by Sandra Widener
Illustrated by Will Terry

2 Genre: Myth

King Midas
and
His Gold

by Patricia and
Fredrick McKissack

Illustrated
by Josée Masse

3 Genre: Nonfiction

Gold
and Money

209

Fox and His Big Wish

by Sandra Widener
illustrated by Will Terry

Fox wanted a snack.
He wished for a big, fresh fish.

Ping!
Fox got his wish!

The fish was big.
It was too big for a snack.

Fox's fish was too big for his dish.
It was too big for his mat.

His fish was not a fresh fish now.
It smelled bad!

Fox did not like his big fish.
He wished that fish was small.

Fox did not get his wish.
That fish went in the trash!

Focus Skill

 Setting

The **setting** is when and where the story takes place.

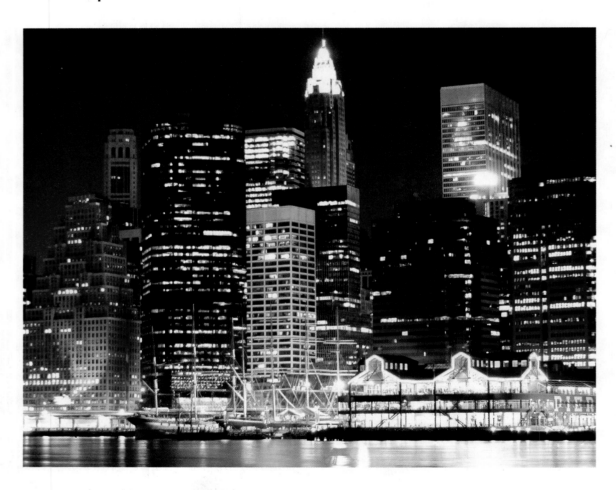

Look at the picture.

The setting is a city at night.

Tell about this picture. What is the setting? How can you tell?

Look at the picture. Choose the words that name the setting.

- a day at the zoo

- an evening at the beach

- a day at the park

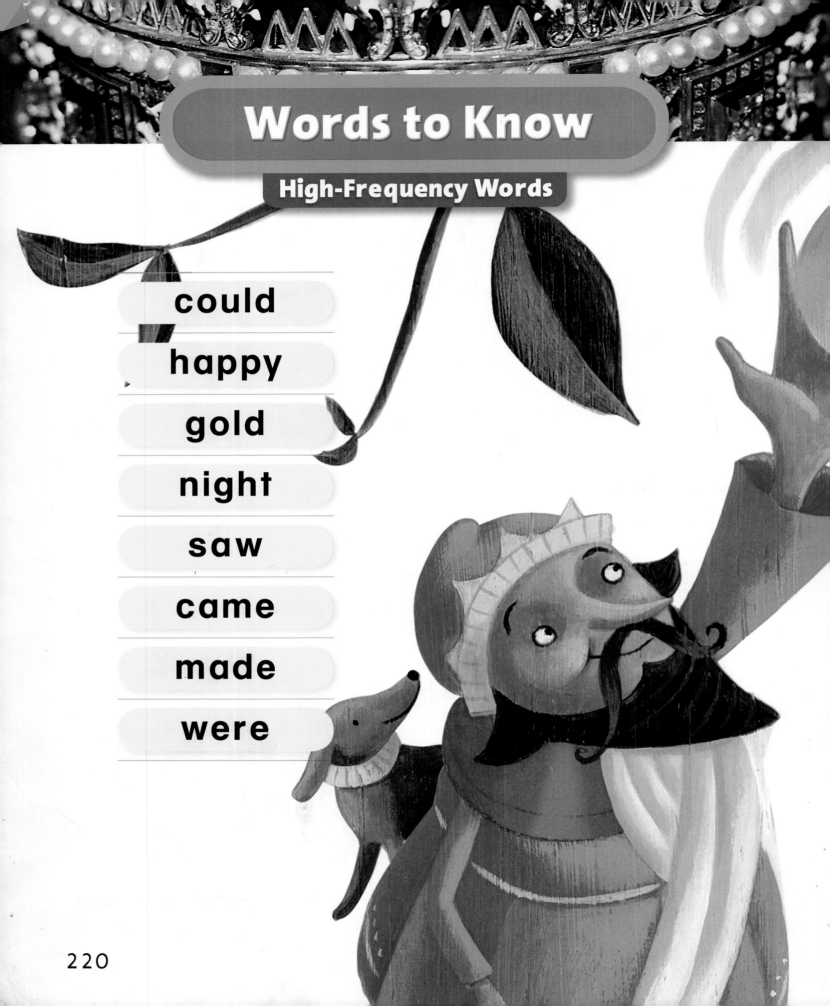

Words to Know

High-Frequency Words

- could
- happy
- gold
- night
- saw
- came
- made
- were

The king asked, "What **could** make me **happy**? Will this **gold** apple make me happy?"

That **night**, the king **saw** a dog. The dog **came** up to him. It licked the king's hand. This **made** the king grin. From then on, they **were** very happy!

 www.harcourtschool.com/storytown

King Midas and His Gold

by Patricia and Fredrick McKissack

illustrated by Josée Masse

Myth

Genre Study

A **myth** is an old story that teaches a lesson. It has make-believe characters and events.

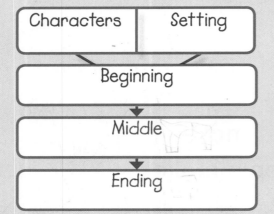

Characters	Setting

Beginning

Middle

Ending

Comprehension Strategy

Ask Questions As you read, ask yourself questions and look for the answers. Where does King Midas get gold?

King Midas
and
His Gold

**by Patricia and
Fredrick McKissack**

illustrated by Josée Masse

Midas was king, but he wasn't happy.
"I wish for gold," he said. "That will
make me happy."

Ping!
The king got his wish.

King Midas picked a fresh apple.
Ping!
In a flash, it was gold.

Ping! Ping! Ping! Ping!
His cup, dish, box, and shelf
were gold.

King Midas felt happy. He had
more and more gold!

King Midas saw a red flower.
Ping! It was gold. King Midas
did not like that.

The king's dog rushed up to him.

Ping! His dog was gold. King Midas
did not like that at all.

King Midas was king, but
he was not very happy. He
could not eat a thing.

Ping! Ping!
King Midas could not rest at night.
His blanket and his bed were gold.

Ping! His pet cat was gold.
Ping! The queen was gold.

"Get back!" cried the king.
"GET BACK!"

Ping!
The princess was gold.
The king was shocked!

All he had was gold and more gold!
King Midas felt very sad.
"I wish for no more gold," he said.
He got his wish.

Ping!
Back came the princess, the queen,
his cat, his dog, the flower, the
apple, and all of his things!

King Midas could eat and rest.

"No more gold," he said, and
this made him happy.

Think Critically

1 How can you tell that this story takes place long ago? SETTING

2 What happens to the apple when the king touches it? DETAILS

3 Why doesn't the king like it when his dog turns to gold? MAKE INFERENCES

4 Why is King Midas glad to lose his golden touch? DRAW CONCLUSIONS

5 **WRITE** Write about something you wish for and tell why. WRITING RESPONSE

Meet the Authors

Patricia and Fredrick McKissack

Patricia and Fredrick McKissack met when they were teenagers. Before they began writing books together, Fredrick owned a construction company. Patricia was a teacher. They especially like to write books that show how a person solves a problem.

Meet the Illustrator
Josée Masse

Josée Masse started drawing when she was very young. Her father was a painter. As a child, she would draw with him in his studio.

Josée Masse has pets—a dog, a cat, many fish, and things her daughter brings from outside, like bugs!

 www.harcourtschool.com/storytown

Gold and Money

The United States has a golden coin.
It is worth one dollar.

front

back

It shows Sacajawea. Long ago,
she helped explorers find
their way across America.

244

Each state has a special quarter. The pictures show things that are important to that state.

Florida Quarter

front

back

Connections

Comparing Texts

1 Do you think King Midas would want the coins from "Gold and Money"? Why or why not?

2 What do you think makes people happy?

3 Tell about a place that makes you happy. Why are you happy there?

Writing

Write Happy on one side of a chart and Sad on the other. List the things that you think make King Midas happy and sad.

Happy	Sad
drink	gold food
rest	gold dog
family	gold bed

Phonics

Make and read new words.

Start with **<u>hut</u>**.

Add $\boxed{\text{s}}$ in front of $\boxed{\text{h}}$.

Change $\boxed{\text{s}}$ $\boxed{\text{h}}$ to $\boxed{\text{r}}$.

Change $\boxed{\text{t}}$ to $\boxed{\text{s}}$ $\boxed{\text{h}}$.

Change $\boxed{\text{r}}$ to $\boxed{\text{w}}$ and $\boxed{\text{u}}$ to $\boxed{\text{i}}$.

Fluency Practice

Read the story aloud with classmates. Look for exclamation points. Use your voice to show excitement and other strong feelings.

Ping! The king got his wish.

Glossary

What Is a Glossary?

A glossary can help you read a word. You can look up the word and read it in a sentence. Each word has a picture to help you.

gift   **Jill got a gift.**

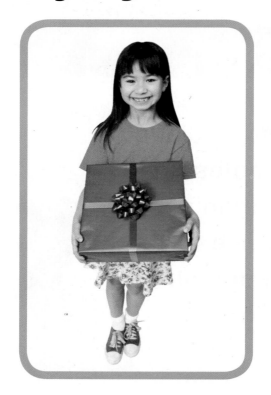

animals   The **animals** have fur.

arms   She is holding out her **arms.**

C

cold   My hands are **cold!**

D

day   We run all **day.**

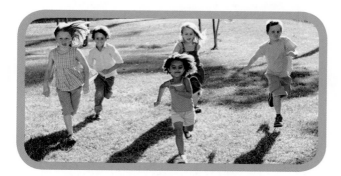

E

eat   This snack is good to **eat.**

feet   Here are my **feet.**

fish   The **fish** is in the water.

food   Look at all the **food!**

gold   The girl has **gold.**

grow   I **grow** a little every day.

happy   Jack is so **happy!**

head   I have a hat on my **head.**

L

line   I made a **line** with string.

N

new   She got something **new.**

night   He went to bed last **night.**

school This is my **school.**

time What **time** is it?

U

under   She is **under** it.

W

water   We splash in the **water.**

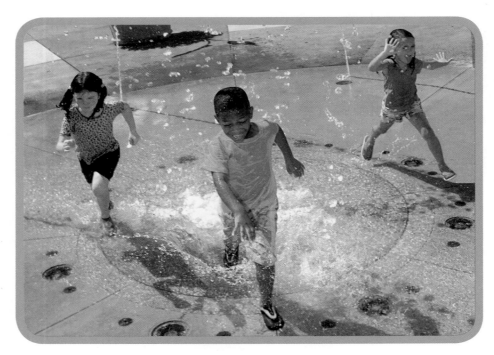

Acknowledgments

For permission to reprint copyrighted material, grateful acknowledgment is made to the following sources:

Curtis Brown, Ltd.: Adapted from *King Midas and His Gold* by Patricia and Fredrick McKissack. Text copyright © 1986 by Regensteiner Publishing Enterprises, Inc.

Harcourt, Inc.: "My Father's Feet" from *Antarctic Antics: A Book of Penguin Poems* by Judy Sierra. Text copyright © 1998 by Judy Sierra.

Lee & Low Books Inc.: "Cornfield Leaves" from *Children of Long Ago* by Lessie Jones Little. Text copyright © 2000 by Weston W. Little, Sr. Estate; text copyright © 1988 by Weston Little.